Sound in the Real World

by Rita Milios

Content Consultant
Julia Vogel, PhD
Science Education Consultant

CORE
LIBRARY

Published by ABDO Publishing Company, PO Box 398166, Minneapolis, MN 55439. Copyright © 2013 by Abdo Consulting Group, Inc. International copyrights reserved in all countries. No part of this book may be reproduced in any form without written permission from the publisher. The Core Library™ is a trademark and logo of ABDO Publishing Company.

Printed in the United States of America,
North Mankato, Minnesota
112012
012013
♻ THIS BOOK CONTAINS AT LEAST 10% RECYCLED MATERIALS.

Editor: Karen Latchana Kenney
Series Designer: Becky Daum

Cataloging-in-Publication Data
Milios, Rita.
 Sound in the real world / Rita Milios.
   p. cm. -- (Science in the real world)
Includes bibliographical references and index.
ISBN 978-1-61783-794-4
1. Sound--Juvenile literature.   I. Title.
534--dc21
                                          2012946821

Photo Credits: Steve Mann/Shutterstock Images, cover, 1; Darin Echelberger/Shutterstock Images, 4; Shutterstock Images, 7, 32, 38; Hulton Archive/Getty Images, 8; Mansell/Time Life Pictures/Getty Images, 10; Andreas Gradin/Shutterstock Images, 14; Red Line Editorial, 16; EpicStockMedia/Shutterstock Images, 17; Yuri Arcurs/Shutterstock Images, 20; Joanna Cameron/DK Images, 22; Michael Higdon, The Tahoe Tribune/AP Images, 24; Christine Gonsalve/Shutterstock Images, 26; Time Life Pictures/Getty Images, 28; Vitalijs Barisevs/Shutterstock Images, 30, 45; Itsuo Inouye/AP Images, 35; Dr. Morley Read/Shutterstock Images, 36; Martin Bureau/AFP/Getty Images, 40

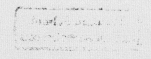

CONTENTS

CHAPTER ONE

What Is Sound?

Imagine that you are standing by an empty railroad track. Notice how quiet it is all around you. But then you begin to hear a sound in the distance. A train is coming. As the train moves toward you, you hear many different sounds. You hear the noise of the train as its cars rattle along the track. You hear the sound of the wind rushing by. Then you hear a loud, shrill sound as the train's whistle blows.

You can hear a train coming from far away.

Listen for the Wave

Sound energy travels in waves. When these energy waves hit our ears, we hear sounds. Sound can travel through solid things such as walls or steel. But sound passes through air more easily. With dense objects, some of the sound waves bounce back. This is the sound of an echo.

Pitch describes how high or low a sound seems to a listener. The speed of a sound wave's vibration is its frequency. Faster vibrations create higher pitches. Slower vibrations create lower pitches.

Sound in Today's World

Sounds are all around us. Inside your home, you may hear sounds from a refrigerator running. When you go outside,

Ultrasound

Ultrasound machines have been used in medicine since the 1950s. They help doctors see inside a person's body. Ultrasound vibrations send sound waves into the body. The waves bounce off human tissue. The returning sound waves can be seen as a picture.

A fire alarm issues a loud sound to warn people of a fire.

you may hear the sounds of birds chirping. Music is sound made by instruments and voices. Some sounds give us warnings, such as sirens or whistles. Sound is important in all areas of our lives. It helps us understand and make use of many things in the world.

PYTHAGORAS.

ΠΥΘΑΓΟΡΗϹ CAMIΩN

Apud Fulvium ...

CHAPTER TWO

The Study of Sound

One of the first people to think about sound in a scientific way was Pythagoras. He lived in ancient Greece in the 500s BCE. Pythagoras noticed that when stringed instruments were played, vibrations were produced. He saw that the vibrations changed when shorter or longer strings were plucked. He noted that each string made a different sound. Pythagoras's work led him to discover that music

Pythagoras was a mathematician and philosopher from Samos in ancient Greece.

Aristotle observed how sound affected different animals.

sounds different depending on how fast sound vibrates. Pythagoras found that shorter strings vibrated faster and made higher-pitched sounds than longer strings.

Around 350 BCE Greek philosopher Aristotle further investigated sound and vibration. He reasoned that sound needs something to travel through, such as air. He described how frequency works. Around the same time French mathematician Marin Mersenne experimented with echoes and the vibrations of stretched strings. The results of his studies became the basis for our understanding of acoustics. Acoustics are the properties of a room or building that are affected by sound waves.

By 1660 CE scientist Robert Boyle experimented with sound in a vacuum. A vacuum is a container with no air inside. Boyle's experiments demonstrated that a medium was needed for sound to travel through.

Further Study

Scientists worked to discover how fast sound waves move. In 1740 Italian scientist G. L. Bianconi found that sound's speed increases when the temperature is higher. And around the same time, the Academy of Sciences in Paris made the first precise measurement of the speed of sound.

In 1842 Christian Doppler found that sound is heard differently when it moves toward or away from a person who is standing still. This is called the Doppler effect. Hermann von Helmholtz made important discoveries about pitch and volume. His book *On the Sensations of Tone* was published in 1863.

In the years that followed, many important scientists have studied the way sound moves and how it is heard. Their discoveries led to a better understanding of sound and technologies that use or create sound.

The Doppler Effect

Have you ever heard a siren on an ambulance as it drives by you? The sound changes pitch as the ambulance gets closer and then moves farther away. This change is called the Doppler effect. Coming toward you, sound waves are squeezed together. So the sound has a higher pitch. After it goes past, the sound waves spread out. Because of this, the sound's pitch is lower.

Read this section from Aristotle's book *The History of Animals*. In it he records his observations of animals and their sounds. This passage is about sounds and how they affect dolphins:

> *For they are observed to run away from any loud noise . . . by the way, though a sound be very slight in the open air, it has a loud and alarming [sound] to creatures that hear under water. And this is shown in the capture of the dolphin; for when the hunters have enclosed a [school] of these fishes with a ring of their canoes, they set up from inside the canoes a loud splashing in the water, and by so doing induce the creatures to run in a [sandbar] high and dry up on the beach, and so capture them while [unable to move] with the noise.*

> Source: Aristotle. D'Arcy Wentworth Thompson, trans. The History of Animals. London: John Bell, 1907. Web. Accessed October 17, 2012.

Back It Up

Aristotle used evidence to support a point in this passage. Write a paragraph describing the point Aristotle is making. Then write down two or three pieces of evidence Aristotle used to make his point.

CHAPTER THREE

Understanding Sound

Differences in sound waves produce different sounds. Sound waves vary in size and shape. These differences may result in higher or lower pitches. Or they may change the volume of a sound. The volume of a sound is its sound intensity. If the volume is high, the sound is loud. This is measured in decibels (dB). The softest sound that a human with

Music has both high and low pitches and is played at a loud volume at a concert.

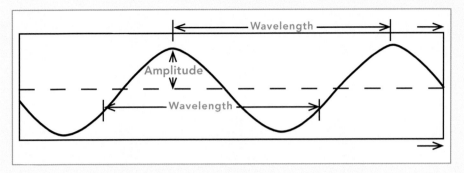

A Sound Wave
This diagram shows what a sound wave looks like. A sound wave is also described in the text. Does the diagram help you understand what a sound wave is like? Is the diagram similar to what is described in the text? In what ways are the diagram and text different?

normal, healthy hearing can hear is measured at 0 dB. Normal conversation measures around 60 dB.

Parts of a Sound Wave

A sound wave looks a bit like an ocean wave. It has crests, or high points, and troughs, or low points. The distance from the top of one crest to the top of the next crest is a wavelength.

The frequency of a sound is the number of wavelengths that pass a given point in a second. It is how fast the wave flows. Sound frequency is

An ocean wave has a similar shape to a sound wave.

measured in hertz (Hz). Sounds are vibrations. A single vibration is when a sound wave moves back and forth across a middle point. One vibration that happens per second is equal to 1 Hz of frequency. Two vibrations per second are equal to 2 Hz.

Heinrich Hertz

In the late 1800s German scientist Heinrich Hertz was the first to send and receive radio waves. The hertz was named after this scientist in 1933.

Amplitude is the height of a sound wave. It determines how loud or soft a sound seems to our ears. Louder sounds have higher-amplitude waves. Softer sounds have lower amplitude waves.

Guglielmo Marconi was an Italian inventor. In 1901 he made a device to send the first radio messages across the Atlantic Ocean. Marconi said of his invention:

> It was shortly after midday on December 12, 1901, . . . that I placed a single earphone to my ear and started listening. . . .
>
> . . . Suddenly, about half past twelve there sounded the sharp click of the "tapper". . . . Unmistakably, the three sharp clicks corresponding to three dots sounded in my ear. . . . "Can you hear anything, Mr. Kemp?" I asked, handing the telephone to my assistant. Kemp heard the same thing as I. . . . The electric waves which were being sent out from Poldhu [Cornwall, England] had travelled the Atlantic. . . .

Source: Degna Marconi. My Father, Marconi. Tonawanda, NY: Guernica Editions, 2001. Print. 93.

Consider Your Audience

Read the passage above closely. How could you adapt Marconi's words for a modern audience, such as your neighbors or your classmates? Write a blog post giving this same information to the new audience. What is the most effective way to get your point across to this audience? How is language you use for the new audience different from Marconi's original text? Why?

CHAPTER FOUR

Sound and Human Hearing

Sound waves are all around, but how do we hear them? The sense organ for hearing is the ear. The outer part of your ear gathers sound waves from the air. It funnels them into the inner ear. Between the outer and middle ear is a small piece of tissue. This is the eardrum. It stretches across the ear canal. The eardrum vibrates when sound waves hit it.

We hear music with sense organs in our ears.

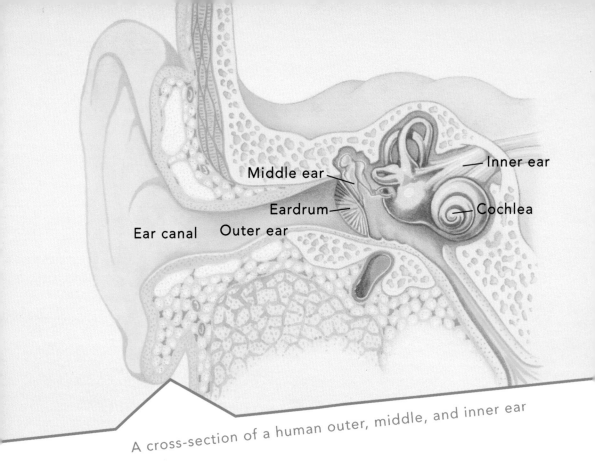

Middle ear

Inner ear

Eardrum

Cochlea

Ear canal   Outer ear

A cross-section of a human outer, middle, and inner ear

Three tiny bones are in the middle ear. These bones pick up sound vibrations. They pass the vibrations to the inner ear. In this deepest area is the cochlea. This hearing organ detects sound vibrations. The vibrations are changed into nerve impulses. Then the nerve impulses are sent to the brain. When the brain receives the nerve impulses, it interprets them as sounds that you can understand.

Hearing Aids and Implants

Some people are born with hearing loss or deafness. Others lose hearing through aging, accidents, or damage because of noisy environments. Sometimes hearing aids can help. These devices are worn in or around the ear. They make sounds louder and easier to hear. Many hearing aids work by using a tiny microphone. It gathers sounds from the air. Then it changes sound waves into electrical signals. The electrical signals are strengthened and sent to a speaker that is worn in the ear canal. A hearing aid only makes sounds louder. If the cochlea is damaged, a hearing aid will not help.

High and Low Ranges

Humans cannot hear sounds at every frequency. The range of hearing for a healthy adult is 20–20,000 Hz. By contrast, dogs and cats have a much broader range of hearing. Cats can often hear between 100–32,000 Hz. Dogs can hear 40–46,000 Hz. Dog whistles make a sound that dogs can hear, but people cannot.

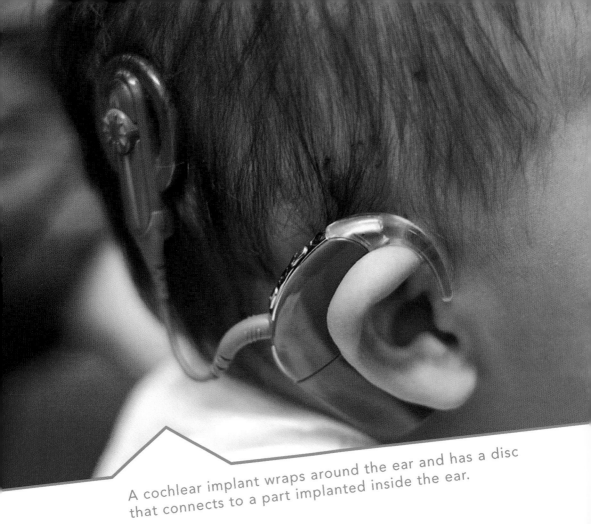

A cochlear implant wraps around the ear and has a disc that connects to a part implanted inside the ear.

In the early 1980s a whole new technology was developed that could help people with damaged cochleae. A cochlear implant takes the place of the damaged cochlea. It uses a small electronic device to change sound waves into vibrations. The vibrations are sent directly to the main hearing nerve. To use a cochlear implant, a doctor must implant one part of the device inside the inner ear. Another part sits outside the ear, much like a hearing aid. The implant picks up different sound wave frequencies.

EXPLORE ONLINE

The focus in Chapter Four was how sound is heard by humans. It also touched upon hearing aids and cochlear implants. The Web site below focuses on cochlear implants. As you know, every source is different. How is the information given in the Web site different from the information in this chapter? What information is the same? How do the two sources present information differently? What can you learn from this Web site?

Cochlear Implants
www.kidshealth.org/parent/general/eyes/cochlear.html

CHAPTER FIVE

Noise Pollution

Sounds that seem unpleasant or unwanted are called noise. Noise can be annoying. But noise to one person is not always noise to another. Some people think certain kinds of music are noise. But others enjoy these same sounds.

One of the loudest noises that people may hear comes from a sonic boom. Some planes, such as military jets, can make a sonic boom. The speed of

Digging up concrete on the road makes a loud noise.

Test pilot Chuck Yeager made history when he broke the sound barrier.

sound is 770 miles per hour (1,238 km/h). When a jet flies faster than the speed of sound, it breaks the sound barrier. Sound waves made by the jet cannot get out of the way of the jet. As the jet flies through its own sound waves, lots of energy is released with a loud boom. On October 14, 1947, Chuck Yeager was the first pilot to officially break the sound barrier.

Can Sound Hurt My Ears?

Uncomfortable noise can also be harmful. This kind of noise is noise pollution. It comes from things such as road noise, airplanes, and trains. It can also come from construction sites. In 1972 the Noise Pollution and Abatement Act became a law in the United States. It established standards to limit noise, protect human health, and limit annoyance to the public.

Noise pollution can interfere with sleep. It is known to cause stress, anger, and frustration. It has been linked to high blood pressure, headaches, and other health problems.

Noise pollution can also lead to hearing loss.

Peaceful Noises

Not all noise is bad. White noise is background noise that can mask other noises. The sound of rain is one example. A humming fan is another. Some people play white noise sounds on a music player to help them fall asleep.

Rock concerts can damage your ears.

Very loud sounds can damage cells in the cochlea.
The damage can become permanent if a person is
exposed to loud sounds over long periods of time.
Noise below 85 dB is usually safe. But there is a risk
for hearing loss at 85 dB or higher.

Rock concerts and crowded sporting events
can have unsafe levels of noise. Motorcycles,
snowmobiles, or other loud vehicles can make noise
at high levels too. One of the greatest dangers to

Quiet Sounds			Loud Sounds		
Sound Source	Decibels	Recommended Exposure Limits	Sound Source	Decibels	Recommended Exposure Limits
Quiet sound	0	Any length of time	School cafeteria	85	8 hours
Empty classroom	35–40	Any length of time	Band class	90	2 hours
Typical library	40	Any length of time	Snowmobile	100	15 minutes
Normal speech	60	Any length of time			

Decibel Scale

This chart shows the decibels put out by different sounds. It also shows how long people should listen to different sounds without damaging their ears. Compare the information shown in the chart above with the information in this chapter. In what ways are both sources similar? In what ways are they different?

hearing comes from using earbuds. Loud music and gaming noises can be very damaging, especially when the source is right next to the ears.

CHAPTER SIX

Sound in the Animal Kingdom

Animals can hear sounds that humans can't hear. Elephants and certain other animals can hear sounds that are very low, called infrasounds. Whales, dolphins, bats, and other animals can hear sounds that are very high. These very high sounds are called ultrasounds. Orcas can hear both very low and very high sounds. They can hear from as low as 0.5 Hz to as high as 100 Hz.

Elephants make and hear very low sounds.

Whales and Dolphins

Whales and dolphins use sound to help them find their way. Dolphins and some whales use echolocation. They send out clicks and other sounds. These sounds bounce off objects. They return to the animal as echoes. Whales and dolphins use the echoes to know where objects are in the water.

Most sounds that orcas send out average around 80 Hz in frequency. Dolphins average 40 Hz. Dolphins don't have vocal cords like people have. Instead, they make their clicks in their nasal passages. The returned echo vibrations

Humpback Whale Songs

Scientists have studied humpback whales for a long time. In 1967 scientists Roger Payne and Scott McVay discovered that male humpback whales create complex vocal sounds, called songs. In 1975 a long-term study of humpback whales began in Hawaii to help scientists learn more about these animals and their use of sound.

Male humpback whales sing complex songs.

Many bats use the echoes of sounds to find their way in the dark.

first enter through their jaws. Then the sound vibrations move to their ears.

Bat Sounds

Many species of bats also use echolocation. Bats use it to hunt insects at night. They also use it to avoid running into things as they fly. Some bats do not see very well. Echolocation helps them find their way in the dark.

Many bat sounds are ultrasonic. They are above the range of human hearing (more than 20,000 Hz). Bats make clicking sounds too. They use the echoes from these sounds to know about the world around them.

FURTHER EVIDENCE

There is quite a bit of information about animal sounds in Chapter Six. It covered the sounds made by elephants, whales, dolphins, and bats. But if you could pick out the main point of the chapter, what would it be? What evidence was given to support that point? Visit the Web site below to learn more about dolphin sounds. Choose a quote from the Web site that relates to this chapter. Does this quote support the author's main point? Does it make a new point? Write a few sentences explaining how the quote you found relates to this chapter.

The Secret Language of Dolphins

www.kids.nationalgeographic.com/kids/stories/animalsnature/dolphin-language/

CHAPTER SEVEN

Sound Technology

S ound is useful in many different machines. It is used in medicine. Sound technology is also used in ships. Special sound equipment tells whether objects in the water are near ships. Sonar is one way sound is used on ships and submarines.

There are two kinds of sonar that ships use. Active sonar sends out sound waves. The sound waves reflect back as echoes. This information is sent

Large ships may use sound to find objects in the water.

A submarine crew listens to sonar to know what is in the water around the ship.

to a computer. The distance of an object is found by measuring the time it takes for the echo to return. The computer can create an image based on the echoes. This image is like a map of the area.

Passive sonar does not send out waves. It picks up sound waves coming toward a ship. It is used mostly to find objects in the water. Submarines may use this kind of sonar.

Another use of sound technology is in music. Musicians use computers and software to create, store, and record music. Sounds of different musical instruments can be mixed using a computer.

Amplifiers are in stereos, televisions, computers, and musical equipment. They are used to increase the volume of sound coming from a machine or instrument. Amplifiers change electrical signals into sound waves.

Sound helps us learn about the world. It helps us communicate, and it warns us of danger. Sound is all around us every day.

Synthesizers

Synthesizers are electronic musical devices. The first synthesizer available for people to buy came out in 1966. Synthesizers change sound waves to electrical signals. Then the waves are changed to sound waves.

IMPORTANT DATES

500s BCE
Pythagoras experiments with sound.

350 BCE
Aristotle makes a theory that sound needs something to travel through.

1660 CE
Scientist Robert Boyle experiments with sound in a vacuum.

1740
Scientist G. L. Bianconi finds that sound's speed increases when the temperature is higher.

1842
Christian Doppler discovers the Doppler effect.

1901
On December 12 Guglielmo Marconi sends the first radio messages across the Atlantic Ocean.

1947
On October 14 Chuck Yeager is the first pilot to officially break the sound barrier.

1966
The first commercial modern synthesizer is released.

1967
Roger Payne and Scott McVay discover the complex songs of male humpback whales.

1972
The Noise Pollution and Abatement Act, which limits public noise pollution, becomes US law.

OTHER WAYS YOU CAN FIND SOUND IN THE REAL WORLD

Emergency Sirens

Ambulance sirens tell car drivers to move out of the way. Emergency sirens in communities sound warnings if tornadoes or other dangers are near. In some newer cars, alarms sound to warn drivers that an object is behind them when backing up. Listen for the alarms in your community. What do they warn you about?

Orchestra Acoustics

Have you heard a professional orchestra play in a concert hall? Most concert halls are designed to have good acoustics. Different features in the hall help sound travel from the stage out to the entire audience. Look up and to the sides of a concert hall. Different panels or sections of the room help sound move in different directions. The design of the room helps create the best possible sound for listeners. Most large cities have orchestra and concert halls. Visit one to hear how acoustic design affects sounds.

The Whalesong Project

Do you wonder what whale songs sound like in the ocean? The Whalesong Project Web site lets you listen to whale songs in real time. The songs are recorded with an underwater microphone. It sends radio signals of the songs to a control center on Maui, Hawaii. Then the songs are sent out on the Internet. Visit the site and click on the Whalesong livestream. Go to www.whalesong.net.

Take a Stand

This book focuses on how sound is made, heard, and used. It also gives some information about animal sounds. Which of these animal sounds was most interesting? Why? Write a short essay explaining your opinion. Include your reasons for your opinion, and give some facts and details to support those reasons.

Another View

There are many sources online and in your library about sound. Ask a librarian or other adult to help you find a reliable source on sound. Compare what you learn in this new source and what you have found out in this book. Then write a short essay comparing and contrasting the new source's information on sound to the ideas in this book. How are they different? How are they similar? Why do you think they are different or similar?

Why Do I Care?

This book explains how sound is heard and used every day. List two or three ways that you use sound in your life. What sounds warn you of danger? What sounds seem like noise pollution? What sounds are nice to hear?

Surprise Me

The study of sound can be interesting and surprising. What two or three facts about sound did you find most surprising? Write a few sentences about each fact. Why did you find them surprising?

GLOSSARY

amplitude
the height of a sound wave

cochlea
part of the inner ear where sound vibrations change into nerve impulses

decibel
unit of measurement for volume of a sound

Doppler effect
an increase or decrease in a sound's frequency as the source moves toward or away from the listener

echolocation
locating objects by listening for sounds that bounce off the objects

frequency
the number of wavelengths that pass a given point in a second

hertz
unit of measurement for sound wave frequency, or pitch of sound

infrasound
a sound wave with a frequency that is too low for humans to hear

sonar
a device that uses sound to find objects underwater

sound waves
a wave, or series of vibrations, through air or other medium

ultrasound
a sound wave with a frequency that is too high for humans to hear

LEARN MORE

Books

Hawkins, Jay. *Super Sonic: The Science of Sound.* New York: Windmill Books, 2013.

McGregor, Harriet. *Sound.* New York: Windmill Books, 2011.

Riley, Peter. *Sound.* Mankato, MN: Sea-to-Sea Publications, 2011.

Web Links

To learn more about sound, visit ABDO Publishing Company online at **www.abdopublishing.com**. Web sites about sound are featured on our Book Links page. These links are routinely monitored and updated to provide the most current information available.
Visit **www.mycorelibrary.com** for free additional tools for teachers and students.

INDEX

ABOUT THE AUTHOR

Rita Milios has published more than 30 books plus numerous curriculum supplements for national publishers. A long-time member of the Society of Children's Book Writers, Milios is a frequent speaker at writers conferences, professional associations, and school events.